DEAL POETS

Tides and Times

An Anthology

Tides and Times
An Anthology
Deal Poets Society

First published in Great Britain 2022

Cover image, *Gilded Flotilla,* by kind permission of Francesca Howard (www.francescahowardartist.com)

We are a group of friends who initially met at creative writing sessions in Deal. Although the class focused mainly on prose, it became apparent that several members of the group were also writing poetry. We decided to meet separately to explore our work in this genre, and so Deal Poets Society was born. The idea for producing a volume of our collected works developed from these gatherings, and *Love, Life, Loss*, our first Anthology, was published in 2019. *Tides and Times* is our second collaboration.

Website https://dealpoets.uk

CIP catalogue record for this title is available from the British Library

ISBN 978-1-915292-50-6

Printed by Biddles Books Limited in Palatino Linotype 11pt

CONTENTS

Foreword

I was delighted to be asked to write the foreword to the second Deal Poets Society anthology, *Tides and Times*. I myself run a poetry club in Walmer and know the challenges involved. The rewards, however, are the extraordinary moments of comradeship and illumination which appear unbidden in meetings; a kind of collective poetic intelligence which gathers and surrounds us in the drawing room of a Sunday morning.

Our group goes by the name of the Walmer Soup-slurping, Stilt-walking, Sherry-sipping Poetry Club; so called because these extraneous activities temper bardic outpourings and bring us back to earth to some extent, and more importantly perhaps, keep us grounded in humour and entertainment. Poetry is not life, rather a window onto it, or a mirror of it. It's worth noting that following the introduction of Sherry-sipping, membership doubled!

A point that often springs to mind in present times is, does poetry have a function, a future now, other than to lightly please or entertain? It once gave, did it not, inspiration, solace, sorrow, joy, moral guidance. 'If you can keep your head when all about you…' It once declaimed, told histories, mighty tales of wars, gods, men. Auden says poetry makes nothing happen, it survives in the valley of its saying – it's a way of happening – a mouth.

But these have been and are now desperate times, and the question has a sharply different resonance. The pandemic and now, even more formidably, war, have cast long shadows across our minds, leading to an inevitable loss of certainty, identity and confidence, and a great deal of soul-searching.

It's interesting to read this work alongside the Society's 2019 *Love, Life, Loss*. Largely wrought in lockdown, *Tides and Times* strikes a deeper and more powerful chord throughout, and answers the previous question of purpose as with a wand.

These poems are the direct expression of experience and existential difficulty during a harrowing and life-altering period, when survival as a functioning human being often meant a difficult coming to grips with oneself and one's situation. As such they move, encourage, console and heal. They are a true *vade mecum* in today's world.

– Lord Gawain Douglas, Walmer, April 2022

IRVING BENJAMIN

In the period since our last collection of poems, all of us have lived through troubled times, a theme which recurs in several of the works in this volume.

For me, that time was dominated by the long illness and final passing in 2020 of my dear wife, Cate, and inevitably those experiences are reflected in many of my contributions. I have divided the poems into those '*Before*' and those '*After*' Cate, plus a few more that don't fit into any pattern.

Benj

BEFORE

Mountain Honeymoon

As the carriage edges round wooded curves
  we scour the red-gold trees for bears, eyes childlike wide.
You look for the brown ones and I'll look for black.
Half a mountain below us a silver ribbon glints;
  alongside it an endless freight train
  chugs slowly from coast to coast.
No bears, but never mind, there's always tomorrow:
  this is our adventure,
  and we are in love.
Lake Louise, glass-still, reflects snow-capped peaks
  in impossible cobalt hue;
  we breathe pure icy air, amble along the bank hand in hand,
  stare up at the distant glacier,
  then dine at the chateau, and watch the fast dying light.
Back down to the shore,
  cocooned against October mountain chill,
  we lie together and gaze into deep moonless indigo:
  there's Orion with his sword, there the Great Bear,
  there Polaris, friend to sailors.
Then the magic: the first one takes us by surprise, then – look!
And another – look!
Soon we lose count.
Of course, we know the cause, understand the science:
  autumnal passage of meteor showers
  through the milky way.
But this night, there is no science, only magic,
  for our eyes only:
  each falling star a blessing on our new life.

In The Loop

Tricky pilotage, so not many go there,
  which is good.
First, spot the opening,
  a darker gap between dark banks.
You call out the depths, *1.3, 1.2...*
I peer ahead, hold my breath,
  waiting for the scrape, then
  we're in The Loop.
Tie up to the bank,
  an island in a sea within a sea within a flat land,
  a hundred years from anywhere,
  a lifetime from reality,
  a stitch in time.
Kill the motor, listen to the stillness.
We braai, smoke rising vertical,
  use the incongruous Portaloo,
  replaced daily by a barge,
  because after all, this is green Zeeland, isn't it?
Sated, we lie down in the cockpit,
  port and starboard,
  read until the light fades,
  reach across to touch fingers,
  then wait as day turns to night,
  looking for the first star.
There - look! - and there...
We savour the silence.

The birds have gone to sleep;
  only the gentle slap of a paddle on the water
  as a woman ferries her dog on a surfboard.
Then, as sky turns to indigo,
  and we can no longer count the stars,
  soft guitar music carries across the water
  from an unseen boat: perfect.
Darkness brings the chilled night dew:
  too cool to sleep on deck.
We go below and hold each other close.
We're In The Loop.

Fairy tern

Your daemon finds you,
looks down through the branches,
pure white against the clear blue sky.
Unseen, he follows you as we climb the slopes
to scary peaks above a distant sea,
and is there again as we regain the trees,
waiting for you.
Now you climb only in your mind,
even the stairs a battle,
but still your spirit creature waits,
to lead you to greater heights.

Scanxiety

These are, after all, but shadows:
Man's genius has cut through your body,
  sliced bacon-thin through bones and organs,
  revealing their deep secrets.
Now in darkened rooms men pore over images,
  peering here, pointing there,
  scrolling back and forth
  through the history of your pain,
  trying to predict your future.
You wait at home, eat, sleep,
  watch TV, read books,
  as the days pass without a call.
What can you hope for?
  Too late to wish for 'Normal',
  for the clock ticks only forwards:
  'Stable' is the best hope.
Then the call comes to break the tense wait:
'No change' for you is a good result -
  a no-score-draw, as good as a bonus point win.
So for now you breathe again,
  sleep, give thanks, share the news:
  then life, and treatment, goes on,
  Scanxiety laid to rest.
Until the next time.

For whom, the bell?

For some,
  the sound is muffled in heavy morning mist,
  carried across a sad, rain-sodden field.
Wet raincoats, heads bowed, tears as yet unshed;
Or echoes through old stones, soaked in prayers;
  or sounds to mark the brave blood shed for us.
Each stroke a full stop, to end life's sentence here.

But not in this place, hanging on this wall:
  its tone resounds in brightly painted hall,
  from children's pictures, coloured bright with love.
Above the constant beeping of machines,
  loud applause returns this bell's three chimes.
A painted rainbow stands behind the bell,
  its curve an arch of each one's hopes and pains.
So this bell tolls to mark the pot of gold
  that says for one at least there lives yet hope:
  a comma, not a full stop, in life's arc,
  in which a bell of optimism tolls.
For some.

Glitterball

In our lounge, now seldom used,
  half dozing in the late afternoon sun,
  I look up from my book.
I watch the fireflies parade across each wall
  as the glitterball turns slowly,
  barely moving in the still air.
Each perfect silver florin of reflected light
  plays over pictures, books, cushions,
  things made, things bought, things found,
  shining its follow spot on our small world;
A silent slide show of our life.

Time to sail

"Yet the day came when she told him,
Time to sail, Thomas.
You are my past now, and I am yours.'"
The Mirror and the Light, by Hilary Mantel

Yes, there will be a time,
A time to sail, as we always sailed together,
But no more: then we will sail on other courses,
Our waypoints different, our headings divergent,
Our destinations unknown, the waters uncharted.
But for now, let our eyes meet and our fingers entwine,
Share our present, recall our past,
The isles we sailed, the hills we climbed:
Our final voyage can wait another day.

AFTER

The Queen and I

(The Queen, the Duke, Cate and me)

So how do you choose
 when 30 is your limit?
When you have more family than that,
 and many, many more friends?
At least, I didn't have to worry about
 the Heads of Commonwealth,
 or the Prime Minister,
 or the Archbishop of Canterbury.
And I hadn't fallen out with my grandson,
 and I could sit next to my children
 without fear, or a mask.
Her absentees could watch live on TV,
 but mine received the video later anyway.
And as it turned out, my hard-chosen thirty
 was just enough.
So in the end (for it was an end)
I think we managed pretty well,
Her Majesty and I.

All My Tomorrows

We store all our yesterdays;
some in books, in files, in photographs,
some in memories that fade and rust.
Or half memories that can suddenly leap from nowhere,
no reason, no rhyme:
sitting on a bus in Oxford with our best friends;
waiting in the sun for the ferry to Kerrera
(or was that just in a story);
proposing at a dinner, overlooking the river.
But where can we store our tomorrows?
Because there is no endless supply of tomorrows.
And now, in this present, nothing feels real,
as if there will be no more tomorrows,
only a slow succession of todays, fading into
yesterdays,
to be forgotten like melted snow, leaving only
rusty, tattered, half memories
that will hit us from behind when we least expect.

Empty Air

"I'm sorry, but
the person you are calling is unavailable;
please try later.
Or to leave a message
please speak after the tone..."

But where will it go?
Will all his words fill the empty air?
How long will they float there
  in a salty sea of unanswered voicemails,
  texts, WhatsApps, emails -
  plaintive cries from the Now to the What-Once-Was?
So what's the point, then, what?

Yet still he'll call you
  across the unbridgeable void,
  just out of habit.
Tell you what he did today;
  a funny thing he saw on the street;
  what the grandchild said;
  how well the band played.
And he'll ask 'How was your day?'
Just for comfort.

An illusion of communication
  in empty air.

Footsteps

(for Mike and Cate)

Yesterday,
we walked 1000 steps.
Steps I had taken before,
alone or in different company.
We trod there in the footsteps
of those who walk no longer,
who left no traces on the ground,
but indelible footprints in the mind,
which time and weather cannot wash away.

And tomorrow,
I will tread on stones worn smooth by ancient boots.
But it will still be the feet that left no trace that I will follow,
there, where we went before,
leaving only precious footprints
in the heart.

AND ANOTHER THING ...

By Whose Consent?

What right had I to breach the pristine skin,
To let the foreign air into the hollow cave
  and shine my light into its private dark?
By whose permission stretched those sacred walls
  and ran my hands through slippery virgin coils?
Familiarity, long years, hours and days
  soon dulls the wonder once so dearly held,
  turns nature's miracle to mundane task -
Cut this, stitch that, follow well-trodden steps,
  Primum non nocere, focus on the goal ...
But now, since I have long passed on the fight,
  looking through my records of a life,
  and reading the cards, the letters, little gifts,
  it is no longer organs I can see,
  but human faces, voices from the past,
  anxious husbands freed from mortal fear,
  granted life, or even just a year...
I close my eyes and smile, glad that some Power,
  or maybe simply Chance, bestowed on me
  the privilege once of turning back a tide
  to change the fortunes of a fellow man.
And I give silent thanks for that Consent.

Willow Wood

The willow wood is still:
  only bird song mellows the silence,
  drowns the faint swish from the distant lane.
A child's cry pierces the still air, once, far away, and is gone.
Leaves barely move, dappling the path with afternoon sun.
It is hot. I lean back on a fallen trunk and doze. I am alone.
A twig cracks and I open my eyes.
A man stops further down the track, looks round,
  sits on a stump.
He takes an instrument from its case
 - a euphonium, I think - and plays once, twice.
The birds stop to listen: *Amazing Grace*.
It's right.
He packs the horn, walks down the track, and is gone. Silence.
I close my eyes again.
Was he here, or was it my dream of another, better time?
A sliver of perfection in a sad, slow world.

The Family Circle

I stand in the garden and look up at the stars.
I hold my arms wide and link my fingers.
Can this circle hold the whole world,
  and the stars and the moon and the planets
  and the galaxies and the multiverse?
No. But it can hold everything important to me:
  it can hold my family, and hold them close to my heart.
And as my family grows, I just have to stretch my arms wider,
  because there will always be room for my family.
Close to my heart.

Our World (a Haiku)

The world we live in,
shrunk to the size of a pea,
still holds you and me.

Exodus

(To my great-great grandfather, Joseph)

And I will make thy seed to multiply as the stars of heaven (Genesis 26:4)

Where did he come from?
Who travelled with him?
Did his wife carry the child in her arms?
Did their shoes wear thin on the cold, hard
   winter ground?
From whom did they flee?
What did they leave behind,
 and did they know where they were going?
Who was here to greet them,
 fill in the forms?
But he arrived, settled his family
 in a strange town, in a strange country,
 with odd voices, new words to grasp.
And did they imitate his Yiddish accent,
 mock his mistakes, revile his heritage;
 or was he welcomed into their hearts?
We cannot say: he passed at 99.
And he would never know
 that now, a century later,
 there are a hundred more who have settled,
 like him, strangers in strange lands,
 bearing his name,
 carrying his genes across the planet.
His journey was worth the cold feet.

JILL BURFORD

My collection of poems broadly fits into two categories: the rather bleak "lockdown" poems and those about the natural world which are more upbeat.

It was impossible not to write poems during this extraordinary period we have all endured or in some cases really enjoyed. The peace we experienced in the first lockdown was memorable - when everything stopped – no planes, no cars. The glorious sound of birdsong could be heard everywhere as we sat in our gardens or went on our daily walks.

Living close to the sea was such a blessing, always inspiring. Isolation was a challenge but also a revelation: getting to know myself better but appreciating family and friends so much when we could meet up again.

.

The Mirror is Empty

Gazing blindly at the looking glass
I see no reflection there.
Locked out in lockdown,
my soul, my essence
has been squeezed, repressed.

Once bright, sparkling eyes
are clouded, opaque,
glazed with apathy,
shrouded with fear.
The future seems so utterly unclear.

Acting out a skeleton life,
my mind is closed, tight shut.
Going through the motions,
trying to survive alone,
I wait for the world to turn again.

I Watch the Ocean Breathe

I watch the ocean breathe
heaving a steady rhythm.
Inaudible inhalation
the sea eases back.

Noisy exhalation,
fizzing, hissing waves release
the foaming spew;
spat out along the shingle beach.

Sucking up the pebbles,
the water retreats again.
Rattling breath.
Death rattle.

The Angry Sea

Almost high tide and a fierce swell,
rolling and breaking,
the waves are wild;
seething with anger from the deep.

An unseen beast haunts our land
and taints the air we breathe
Unseen, unchecked, it spreads
fear and misery amongst us all.

Wearing masks, keeping apart,
weeks and months slip by.
We try to do what we are told.
Our normal lives are put on hold.

A Sprinkle of Stardust

On that frosty morning,
I woke with heavy dread.
Hot tears flood my bloodshot eyes
and sad thoughts haunt my head.

A shaft of golden sunlight
pierced the mournful gloom.
Highlighting clouds of dust motes,
swirl round the silent room.

A sprinkle of stardust had been cast,
so colourful and carefree.
Each tiny speck was dancing
and floating gracefully.

I believe your sweet soul
had chosen that very hour
to break loose
and freely soar.

Beach Sketches on Remembrance Day

Skeletal clouds and ghostly outline of the setting moon
faintly etched across the pastel-blue sky.
A vast tangerine sun rising in the east,
its slender rays splash gold over the silken sea.

As a lone seagull bobs happily on the swell,
an earnest chap picks up litter. His white bag billows
in the breeze, like a tiny plastic sail.
Sea-soaked pebbles sparkle in the bright morning light.

Anorak-clad yoga-poses "Salute to the Sun".
Swimmers, with ruddy limbs,
watch as burly fishermen haul their boat
up the steeply banked strand.

Headphone-wearing walkers cannot hear
the gentle lapping of the waves,
the brittle crunch of shingle under their feet
or the urgent calls of gulls above their heads.

A scatty dog, coiled spring of energy,
dashes into the sea to dip his paws;
then charges back again,
tail wagging, tongue lolling.

I bow my head as I walk home,
through Walmer Green, past the bandstand,
swathed with wreaths of vivid red poppies:
Remembering the lives of eleven young bandsmen.

Shadows

Crisp black silhouettes
On stark white buildings
Sunshine is a perfect foil
No hiding place at all

Illuminating dark thoughts
Secrets buried deep
Shadows seek to highlight
What bright light tries to hide

Feeling Blue

Sometimes I feel a bit sad and blue.
Not a pretty blue but a dark, steely grey blue,
that hangs like a heavy curtain of doom.
No-one can help, I know it will pass.

My zest has simply sizzled out.
I have to wait for my energy to lift and then,
I am up again in the wispy fair-weather clouds,
soaring with the birds, on a good day.

When I am Old

When I am old, don't take me out in a motorised chair,
with my crumpled skin and threadbare hair.
A museum piece, wrapped in woolly shawl,
muscles barely there at all.

People peer down to shout, or worse,
poke ghastly baby pap at my clamped-tight jaw.
My teeth long gone. in their place – a gummy mouth
or painful, plastic, rictus row.

Don't ask my grandchildren to kiss a fusty gran,
who once was fun and giggled just like them.

My opaque eyes will have seen
all they ever wanted to see.
My arms will have hugged so much,
they will be quite worn out.
My weary ears won't hear the lark sing
or the cuckoo call.

My treasured memories,
no longer able to recall.

No! Please God – no!
When I am old - I'll be ready to go.

Big Issue!

"Big Issue! Big Issue!
Please buy! Please.
Good morning, Boss"
Calls the man in the street,
Warmly wrapped, but still looks cold
"Big Issue! New one today, Miss."
What is the Big Issue?

People starving, millions homeless
Migrants fleeing from oppression
Our NHS in crisis
Foodbanks .... Everywhere.
The rich getting richer
Brexit? Let's not go there.

Loads of big issues,
too many to record.
Is that the Big Issue?

Our seas swarming with plastic
Icecaps melting, global warming
Our cities dense with pollution
Natural resources depleted
We are destroying our beautiful world.

Is this the *really,* Big Issue?

Birds on a Wire

Perfectly spaced on telegraph wires,
scores of starlings, like notes on a stave.
No time to write a musical transcription,
before they wheel away in flighty formation.

At ground level, a sturdy bird,
with pied head and grey tail bobbing -
glides oddly, automaton-like -
then flies away, with dipping flight.

A lone robin is perched up high,
with brash red chest and treble trill.
He cuts a dash and knows it well
but can be savage and swift to kill.

Sparrows are my favourite bird,
crescendo chirping while they bustle
and flutter with cheerful chatter
or paddle in puddles with feathers fluffed.

Check out the dapper little male:
his bold, black bib and bandit-lined eyes;
smooth Moles' Breath breast
and impressionist-flecked wings.

The Joy of Pear Gleaning

Armed with empty sacks and willing hands,
gleaners gather in the morning mist.
Milky sun peeks through grey cloud sky,
shines weakly down the rows of trees.

Leaves rustle in the gentle drizzle.
The team spreads out – social distance rules.
Tripping over windfalls, slipping on mud,
outwitting wasps, we seek only the best.

Bags fully filled with fragrant sweet fruit;
gathered with love, for all to enjoy.

Webs of Wonder

Miles of fine silk spun into webs of wonder.
Glistening with morning dew.
Stunning beauty, cunningly disguises
the lair of the lethal-jawed beast.

The long-legged, hunchbacked monster, eyes on stalks,
crouches in the shadows and waits,
so patiently, for fly or moth
to collide with this sticky trap.

The fly flutters and flaps, attempts to escape,
but the spider works too fast.
He scuttles out along the thread
and tightly wraps it up.

Intricate lace, worked in a perfect pattern,
strung between hedgerow and tree.
Not a dream catcher.
This is a death snatcher.

FAY FRANKLIN

I've worked and played with words all my life – professionally as a bookseller and non-fiction editor, the rest of the time as a writer of short fiction and poetry. Perhaps that's why these ten poems don't seem to have a lot in common – my jackdaw mind picks up shiny items of inspiration all over the place. But there are some lifelong passions reflected in more than one piece here, including my love of wildlife (and, now, living by the sea), as well as my inability to keep quiet in the face of injustice.

Curiosity and Perseverance

Look at you now, you two.
Making your marks upon a dead terrain,
searching for life.

Strange how it has turned about,
that Curiosity persevered for all these years,
until we sent another –
Perseverance –
curious to see what more we could find out.

One day there will be footsteps in your tracks.
A colony in the dry lakebed that you mapped.
They'll name it Bradbury, perhaps,
in subtle honour.

And you two will be in the town museum –
artefacts.

These are what will take us to stars, you know.
Curiosity and Perseverance.

Three Dawn Choruses

I wake, these days,
to the gruff chunterings of gulls,
interspersed, in spring,
with pitchy squeaks
as little beaks start to appear
amid the shabby gatherings of twigs.

And then, like an alarm,
the sounds grow louder with the dawn.
Those familiar seaside calls -
the back and forth -
accompany my rising and routine:
the feeding of the cat; the kettle; tea;
the hourly news. Their news as well -
a herring boat arriving on the rising tide.

First dawn in the old house
we woke up laughing at the noise.
Green light sifting in through new leaves,
through uncurtained windows -
and the din! Wrens, robins,
blackbirds, thrushes, finches, tits,
dunnocks, and a nameless chorus more.
An unimagined, unexpected welcome.

Once, on the far side of the planet,
jet-lagged and grubby, we'd fallen into bed
only to be disturbed again by hallucinatory sounds.
Mad laughter, rattles, whoops and shrieks.
Aboriginal in origin, dazzling in the half-dark.
Drawing us sleep-walking onto the beach
into the dawn chorus. And, all around us,
rising like rainbows, the birds of another world.

The grace of these dawn choruses,
each one marking another rising sun,
each one so different, each somehow the same,
heralding another unimagined, unexpected day begun.

Selkie, Beached

The water pulls me back.
The water pushes forward more
and now I'm settled here
beached once again upon the shingle shore.

Old bones, old scars,
are warmed by the rising sun.
I adjust my ancient bulk, and rest my head.
The tide acquiesces, its work done.

There is another creature here –
one of those bound tightly to the land –
making quiet comfort sounds
(even though I cannot understand).

Perhaps both of us beached, or both adrift.
It matters not a lot to me.
I care for hunger, fighting, and the breed.
And the sweet siren-calling of the sea.

I am an old warrior, battle-scarred.
Unafraid to look into her eyes,
say, let me lie here, undisturbed.
She doesn't move, watches the sun rise.

My wary sleep remains the same, filled
with blood-vivid memories of when I would
rule triumphant over sea and sand.
Teeth tearing chunks of rivals and of food.

My blood stirs as the tide draws back.
I haul my vastness to the shingle's lee.
She sits there still, makes soft sounds of farewell.
I turn and head into the waves – my home embraces me.

Later, if she sheds salt water,
like the sea,
well, that means nothing much at all
to such as me.

Elegy for an Osprey

(For Monty, and Emyr)

'Such soar, but never set...'
a poet wrote, a century or so ago.
Perhaps she'd smile to know
I've used it in your elegy tonight.

'Is it possible to fall in love
with a wild bird?'
your grieving watchman wrote,
just a few weeks ago.
And ten thousand readers will reply
yes - oh yes - and yes again,
from all around the world, tomorrow.

This has been a labour of love.
His work.
My work.
But your work most of all.

Hard even to conceive the call
that drew you back each year
to Wales from Africa
(The Gambia, or Senegal),
to that same marsh-set nest to breed
and raise your young.

To watch them thrive and fledge.
To spot a flounder or a mullet from a hundred feet
in muddy darkness, with keen amber eyes,
and bring it wriggling, thrashing, back
time after time and time again.

I hope the warm winds of last September
lifted you away from the Welsh rain
and took you to a place of rest.
A soft hollow in the sands of Africa,
your bones warmed by the setting sun.
Your work and all your journeys done.

Soon, your offspring will be greeted here again,
following your route, clear as a guiding light,
taking your place in skies once graced
by your soaring, never-setting, flight.

Sweet Insurrection

(17 June 2020)

This summer evening,
spreading out
across the bone-dry grass,
a circle forms.
Maybe an Osman-length apart
or maybe not.

Old friends - some forty years,
some just a few -
to say farewell.

And Lucy on her bicycle,
bright as a circus girl,
spins round about us -
and if she doesn't do a headstand
on the seat, well, it's magic anyway.

A few faint drops of rainfall
and the setting sun -
"There must be a rainbow somewhere"
someone says (it may be me)
and we look up,
scanning the blue-grey sky
for the invisibility.

The circle holds me close.
After ten solitary weeks
I kiss the soft head
of a dog.
I kiss my departing friend
and hold her in my arms
and say, "I love you".

This is all we have.
Nobody really leaves;
nobody really even dies
that we don't want to lose.

Such a sweet insurrection
against the growing dark.
Against the growing dark invisibility.

Goodnight, Matisse

White muslin, sprigged with flowers,
moves gently in the warm sea breeze.

But you cannot see the sparkle of the ocean
and the blowsy sailboats
beyond your window now.

Like memory, your bright blue eyes
Have faded white as clouds.

The cats are good company
in bed
and pounce
on scraps of paper
from your cut collages,
making you laugh aloud.

I wish I could help you to the window,
push away the curtain and say
"Look, Henri!"
And you could see once more
the Baie des Anges,
and a young woman
waving to you from the shore.

The night air is warm.
Low over the sea,
the harvest moon
tracks a bright pathway
to the artist's door.

It seeks him out,
Pushes past the curtain,
Brushes the heavy scented roses (petals fall)
to paint patterns on his sleeping face.

One of the cats stirs –
gold eyes wax and wane
like the inconstant moon –
then curls back, purring
on her master's chest.
The artist, dreaming colours, smiles.

A Little Second Hand

The tattered, slim, black leather band
around my wrist -
white face with Roman numerals,
gold frame and cabochon -
I wonder whose you were before.

Bought from a junk-shop counter
for a pound or two, only to replace
(just for week or two)
the precious one I always wore.

They tick our time away,
we unaware of the minutes that they mark.
The watches that accompany us
into the dark.

Were you ever plunged,
unthinkingly, into the sea before?
Or did the slim wrist that was yours
wear you out dancing?
Maybe were you slyly checked
through endless meetings,
counting down for her the end of weekday bore.
Had you ever suffered a patting-dry
with salty beach towels on a summer shore?

I'll never know. But you survived it well.
That little second hand kept moving.
And you (a little second-hand,
a temporary timepiece)
kept on ticking – watching, if you will.

Until my own soon-mended watch
slips back around my wrist,
familiar as a lover's hand.
And then you'll be consigned
again into a drawer.

Ticking the time away into the future,
as they have done for all the years before,
always on watch, these timepieces –
never just watches, always something more.

So, Tell Me...

So, tell me –

Did you never hear your footsteps echo
down a midnight street
and pause a moment, only to hear the echo carry on?
And not so very far behind?
And start to walk again, but faster,
but not – oh no – not ever dare to run?

And did you never promise friends,
standing in their cosy, lamp-lit porch,
"I'll text you the minute I get home"?
And if, by chance, forgetting, letting minutes pass,
after you closed your own front door,
receive an anxious message from them on your phone?

And did you never shrink down in your seat
as each stop emptied out the last train home
until the carriage held just you – and him in 15B?
And, when you finally alight,
pray that, as the doors slide closed, he won't step down
onto the shuttered platform – no one else there but you and he?

And did you never, ever, feel the need to do the 'right thing',
but always feel confident to take the short-cut home –
across the park in darkness, three sheets to the wind,
down the unlit alley, past the late-night bars
(maybe stopping in for a swift nightcap) –
sure and certain you'd get home safely in the end?

Congratulations – you're a man, my friend.

The Ghost of Christmas Yet to Come

The Ghost of Christmas Yet To Come
walks early this year down your autumn street
(tattered robes shuffling the dying leaves),
scattering a trail of bitter little sweets.

The Ghost of Christmas Yet To Come
wears a Jack o' Lanterns smile this year,
promising prizes from a spangled bag
and telling tales not fit for little ears.

The Ghost of Christmas Yet To Come
peers into windows as dusk dims the sky,
fogging the panes with his slow, wheezy breath
and catching the curiosity in little eyes.

The Ghost of Christmas Yet To Come
breaks into shambling dances like a circus clown,
plucks paper flowers from a sleeve, that then
fade into dust, provoking little frowns.

The Ghost of Christmas Yet To Come
stalks the dark streets, kicks a blowing mask.
Kicks a shape sleeping in a doorway. Frowns
at his list of tiresome little tasks.

The Ghost of Christmas Yet To Come
descends our chimneys – nothing but a chart
of bad news to clip on waiting bed-ends.
No comfort for the fluttering of little hearts.

The Ghost of Christmas Yet To Come
speaks every night in platitudes from a bright screen.
World-beating lies are pulled like crackers, while we,
his turkeys, can little try to fathom what he means.

Gracious

('For' N.E.)

"Would it be ungracious?" the politician asked.
Rhetorical - she knew the answer - yes it would.
She went to bed, certain the moment past.
And the world turned
like a football spinning off a post.

But, sometimes, the world turns back -
a double-take - and then there are penalties to pay.
And words we say to make ourselves seem smart
come back to sting us harder
the next day.

Because such things as graciousness, and grace -
those qualities we've seen
under duress, these past long months -
have become curiously prized.
So to despise them, to suggest
that 'ungracious' is just a casual jest,
in preface to a sneer,
is such a cold reveal,
showing no care of what a nation feels.

Boys on their knees have more idea of what it takes
to love their fellow beings than most politicians, heaven's sakes.

IAN HINDMARCH

Writing poetry has been a therapeutic activity since my retirement after 40 years of academic medical research and the associated publishing of 'non-creative' scientific papers.
This selection is loosely based on 'endings'. It could be the end of an affair, or of a dream, or of life, or of a career, or of melancholy, or of desire, or of solitude, or ....
I share Falstaff's belief that 'he who laughs last, laughs longest' and much of what follows contains a vein of humour, simply for the joy that brings.

The fairy's funeral

In a magic dell, not of our real world,
but to our daydreamed stories so well known,
lies the tiniest pyre of sweet pinecone
ringed by wood sprites with silver wings tight furled.
Atop a nearby elm tree bole, grey knurled,
an enthroned fairy king mourns quite alone.
His broken heart's as bruised as pummelled stone
and grief filled eyes by tiny tears are pearled.

To grey-white dawn he wails for his dead wife
"I can no longer live without her light
that bright lit all our treasured romances.
Dryads and nymphs spark her again to life
or let me grieve 'till I join that stark night
where dark goblin death leads all the dances".

Escaping the shadows of the dark wood

I had lived in the shadow of the dark wood
where trees, full laden with black fruits of despair,
thrived in a tangled undergrowth of self- doubt
ready to send cloying tendrils of morning melancholy
to trap me in their worthless, smothering folds.

I took refuge from the stalking demons' clouds of black bile
in books and in the arcane wisdom of the ancients,
and discovered hedonistic pleasures with the lotus eaters.
On sunlit hills I partook of the nectar which eases mental pain
and was transported to a carefree, daydream world.

Minarets and domes of Samarkand gleamed on far horizons
and houris danced at my every whim on golden marble floors.
I began to understand my life: gained insight and reason.
The visions eventually ebbed like foamy wavelets
beating retreat on a distant sandy desert shore.
So too the black shadows waned and were then no more.

I was forced back deep into that dark wood.
Commonplace worry and turgid existential angst
impaled me on their rack of mental misery and gloom.
My fair-weather friends stood apart from my distress.

Waking was worse than succubi or night terrors.
Straight jacketed by the black dog of paranoid melancholy,
I no longer felt touched by the sun of life.
The alchemist shaman gave me essence of happiness in a pill.

I reposed fitfully in an anodyne, restless sleep
and, without access to my labyrinthine subconscious,
waked in a medicated, care-less, existence.
A bemused smile played on my lips but didn't reach my eyes.
I had no libido, creative wit, nor flights of mental fancy.
Without imagination my life was a joy-free zone.

Permanent happiness is not man's normal state,
so light me another pipe please, Su Ling.
I need the reverie again

The Moirai.

Since that first curtain raised
and Time's great clock began to tick,
the three Fates, fatherless daughters of Night,
began their task of governing mortal lives.

Clotho spun my thread of life.
Her deft fingers plying wheel and spindle
gave every nuance to my living
held in thrall by twist of yarn.
Some small imperfections required attention
but, by and large, the weft was fine.
The hues and shades of the skeins varied.
Stygian black, mystic purple,
tranquil blue, verdant green,
startling yellow, steamy crimson,
coloured my moods and real-life dreams.

Lachesis allotted my length of thread
to last from birth till The Fates know when.
Through life's labyrinth I follow her strand
and find kindness, hatred, sordid passion, deceit, love.
The stoic's path I tread, stimulates, is never bland.
With crossed fingers I test out Dame Fortune's hand.
I am led through groves of academe to understand
the values of my life in both the mundane and the grand.
She fixes my destiny. Though I've delusions of free will,
my life's path lies in her cat's-cradle: tight, entwined.

Inflexible Atropos, the third daughter, I have not yet met.
She'll grant night perpetual when her shears crop my thread.
Inevitable, she's devoid of humour, immune to pleading.
A cynic who knows not how much fun it is to dine, drink, dance,
and spend languid hours daydreaming in the sun,
listening to the harmonies of the spheres
… snippety snip.
Please! Wait until this perfect cadence falls
… snippety snip.
No! I can't, I've no time, my diary's full
… snippety
SNIP.

That first bite of the apple

Humid air glazed large fronds and leaves.
Mist droplets moistened the firm, pink breasts of Eve's.
Birdsong, humming bees and a tinkling stream
made Eden seem so much like a Disney cartoon dream.

Adam, dozing under a tree, seemed to the world dead
with not a single thought present in his handsome head.
He was an eager gardener, a horticultural overachiever,
but he suffered severely with seasonal hay fever.

He was naïve, even by the standards of times primordial,
and knew nothing of anti-allergy nostrums or cordial.
His runny nose he found it hard to wipe and relieve
for he was without a garment with a suitable sleeve.

Recently Adam had surgery performed on his rib cage
which was a rare occurrence in that day and age.
After the op he'd been in the Doldrums, taken by the lee
with lethargy and low mood, the so-called melancholy.

Suffused with misery from excess of black bile,
he hoped new playmate Eve might amuse him for a while.
She was in the orchard when he saw her from afar,
participating in a tableau, both biblical and bizarre.

Draped thrice round the trunk of a Cox's Orange Pippin
was a suitably satanic serpent with saliva dripping
from its fanged mouth set wide in a knowing smile.
Its devious intentions were evident, even at a mile.

Snake proffered a ripe, rosy fruit to guileless Eve,
who, seduced by serpentine scheming, did it receive.
When Adam arrived, open-mouthed, upon the scene,
he saw Eve was clad in a fig-leaf bikini of deepest green.

She gazed, with her new-found lascivious depravity,
on his exposed, but hitherto unnoticed, masculinity.
'Hey Adam, get your laughing gear round this Cox,
a bite will grant existential awareness, blow your cotton socks'.

'But,' said the number one guy on earth, 'both you and me
have been forbidden to ever touch the fruit of that tree.'
'Yes,'said Eve, 'now I feel embarrassment and shame
and I know some things will never be the same.

You'll see I've covered up my lady bits,
now you'll do anything for a peek at my bum or tits
I know I'll have my own way. With desire you'll groan
with just a flash of my erogenous zone.'

After a mouthful, Adam too gained insight rich.
Eve sashayed up for attention, like a persistent itch.
He resisted all temptation, told Eve to ride her bike away,
twerking was so pointless: Adam was the archetypal Gay.

The Warlock

Adam Bell was irate as could be
and he damned all his witches to hell
as each time he brewed peppermint tea
they complained of its strong herbal smell.

They were enthralled by his arcane lore,
he was an agreeable wizard,
nightly sex games were never a chore
and they dined off finest goose gizzard.

With spells they pestered the parson's pig
and made corpse-reeking cauldrons bubble.
Sore piles were cured with syrup of fig
but mashing mint tea was just trouble.

Adam enjoyed mass fornication,
his coven sported much willing flesh.
He'd served enough to seed a nation,
variety kept him ever fresh.

After bouts of debauched excesses,
he'd play some rubbers of contract bridge.
To reduce existential stresses
he'd drink mugs of iced tea from the fridge.

One night, two young vixens did display
nude tableaux vivants, as amuses bouches
served with glasses of chilled Chardonnay
before sex in threes and fondling louche.

Now, with bottles of burgundy white
- peppermint tea's seen as a baddie -
there are drunken orgies every night,
the herbal stuff's back in the caddy.

Avian dreams

I can't fly, but my pigeons can.
From their loft above the garden shed
they pass house gables, high they soar
above the road and the red mail van
round the churchyard and the 'King's Head'
towards a blue, far-distant shore.

Tricky, Rollo, Bert and Captain Shaw.
Feathers shade from grey to deep blacklead.
All fly as equals, no one's boss.
They rise through dawn-born haw
up to skies where white, puff-clouds are bred,
even higher than the church steeple cross.

Soon the town seems but a brick-red blot
set midst a green and brown patchwork.
Jerky beats of stubby wings cut sun-warmed air,
until, on reaching an unmarked but exact spot,
they orient by an inbred compass quirk,
and turn for home and the cooing wives waiting there.

I can only dream in my earthbound state
what fancy visions and flights of mind
would come to pass if I could fly.
Imagined pleasures I'll find other ways to sate
as with fruit of grape I do unwind
and feast on fresh baked pigeon pie.

Maude, the bearded lady: a pantoum

Paraffin lanterns cast a bright white light
about the striped tent that was her bower.
Maude received clients throughout the long night
'till four struck the clock on the old tower.

About the striped tent that was her bower
souvenirs lay of her freak-show career
'till four struck the clock on the old tower
she watched them gawp, foul-breathed, sweaty and near.

Souvenirs lay of her freak-show career
bright coloured posters, a dried sunflower.
She watched them gawp, foul-breathed, sweaty and near
Maude posed quite naked, armed with a glower.

Bright coloured posters, a dried sunflower
raw memories of dead daughter's sunny smile.
Maude posed quite naked, armed with a glower,
strongman George said he'd loved her for a while.

Raw memories of her daughter's sunny smile
George made tea with cakes and asked her to wed.
Strongman George said he'd loved her for a while.
In front of the fakir their vows were said.

George made tea with cakes and asked her to wed,
she'd been a mother but never a wife.
In front of the fakir their vows were said,
George and the Bearded Lady joined for life.

She'd been a mother but never a wife.
Maude received clients throughout the long night.
George and the Bearded Lady joined for life.
Paraffin lanterns cast a bright white light.

The Season's Instructions

Bind me with spells,
when spring's green buds burst bright on dove-grey branches.

Love with passion,
when summer's sun warms through the open window.

Cuddle comfortably,
when golden-brown autumn leaves tumble in the wind.

Leave me,
when ice-bleak winter takes all, even our breath, away.

The ladies' luncheon club

The Hon. Sec. in tweed two-piece costume,
met him outside the general waiting room
of the railway station.

"Professor Smith, I presume? Here for the talk?
... hall's down here ... just a short walk ...
a convenient perambulation."

Floorboards creaked as the ladies milled about,
anorexic young mums and matrons stout:
a womanly population.

Some made for the speaker with cow eyes, bold as brass.
Hon. Sec. fluttered her eyelids in a subtle pass:
an encouraging flirtation.

Prof. and Hon. Sec. chit-chatted as he sorted his slides
with innuendo laced hints and witty asides
of concupiscent infatuation.

"I'll do the honours today Chair's indisposed,
she sounded awful on the phone, I diagnosed
Chardonnay intoxication.

As for the audience, please don't be concerned,
We're a full house, eager to hear what you've termed
'Platonic transmogrification'.

Let's go now ... there's no queue for the buffet luncheon ...
later I'll find you something else to munch on ...
other than the cold collation...

… you'll join me in a glass of Rhenish wine?
… help the quiche slip down … yes, we've time
… everything in moderation.

Let's sit here, a quiet table set just for two,
I've been looking forward to meeting you
for my personal edification.

I understand you'll be staying locally overnight,
perchance you and I could enjoy the pleasure and delight
of carefree copulation?

Oh, I almost forgot, please sign this docket for your fees,
I've such a passionate trembling in my knees,
I'm pregnant with anticipation."

A rummer full of Blue Nun is neither wine at its best
nor a good way to maintain the necessary zest
for an erudite presentation.

Meanwhile, the Treasurer's erstwhile baking chum
had added too much grog to the *baba au rhum,*
and caused audience stupefication.

The ladies who snoozed through the lecture that day
recalled only bizarre and confused things to relay
about corporeal transmutation.

They'd all dreamt of a tryst: Prof was really a dish.
But none, bar the Hon. Sec., was granted her wish
for Professorial conjugation.

Today, my final lecture of them all
Moscow February 2012

Today, my final lecture of them all,
I hear the wintry cough and shuffled shoe,
I sense again Pavlov's ghost's soft footfall.

My metier was always to enthral,
presenting findings from my research crew.
Today, my final lecture of them all.

Neuroscientists' photos on the wall,
pickled brains of the famous there to view.
I sense again Pavlov's ghost's soft footfall.

Then, before the Soviet Republic's fall,
they'd quizzed me about all I ever knew.
Today, my final lecture of them all.

No KGB girls now in hotel hall,
no more toasts to Peace, no nighttime curfew.
I sense again Pavlov's ghost's soft footfall.

Then 'shampanski' with caviar on call,
and state-owned Stolichnaya with my stew.
Today, my final lecture of them all,
I sense again Pavlov's ghost's soft footfall.

Product placement

Lambrusco and Parmesan

My ever-loving girlfriend Anne,
loved to lunch on old Parmesan.
Down her gullet the cheese would go
with quaffs of sparkling Lambrusco.
Whilst in her stomach they'd make gas
which, in time, leaked out of her ass.
Lovers heed the pleas from my heart
wine with hard cheese makes girlfriends fart.

M&S men's boxer shorts

I'm not fooled by your come-hither beauty,
nor by your seductive singing.
You are a brazen, rock dwelling Siren
who'll never make a swine of me.
I am protected by a talisman.
My undergarments are charmed.
Spun, under the aegis of Saint Michael.

Dizain: Dr. Spooner's Yuletide Dinner, New College, Oxford 1880

Choristers, in surplices starched stiff white,
sing ancient carols at the Christmas Feast.
Beeswax perfume hangs in the candlelight.
Rosemary sprigged head of a forest beast
is welcomed and blessed by the parish priest.
Stomachs gurgle as all there do perceive
the festive food they're about to receive.
Spooner exclaimed when he saw the boar's head,
"there's naught better on a cold winter's eve
than a good helping of a hot whore's bed."

A dizain is a 10 line stanza with 10 syllables per line.
Rhyme scheme is fixed:- ababbccdcd
French, 15-16 century and popular in 1920's and 30's

GEORGINA KOUBEL

During the time that it has taken for this Anthology to reach the light of day, there have been a number of parallels between the universal experience and my particular circumstances. Personal issues of loss and loneliness have been mirrored by what has been occurring across the planet, and vice versa. In addition to my reflections on the pandemic, these poems cover a period of time that for me as an individual has encompassed considerable movement, travelling from a place of sadness and grief via changes and challenges to one where I have gradually reached an acceptance of what has passed, and feel ready to invest in tentative shoots of hope for the future. In the most difficult of times, we become intensely aware of the need to value most deeply the consolations and connections that sustain us.

The pictures that we painted

The pictures that we painted
were grisailled of dreams and shadows.
From gossamer thread and butterfly wings
we wove our rainbow tapestry.

With the aid of poetry,
we made a magic lantern spaceship
that we imagined could transport us
to live among the stars.

We spun our webs of shining words
into worlds of wild intensity:
lightning dancers whirling
to the music of the spheres.

We lived our lives like dragonflies,
distracted by the glitter,
skating on the dazzle,
mating on the wind.

We always knew the carp were circling
just below the surface: with their
upside-down grins, waiting to strike
the moment we forgot them.

Catching the bus
(the dream)

We had been to visit your mother,
and were just heading home,
at the end of the day.
As you do.

Your hand lightly nesting my elbow,
a reassuring pressure,
holding me, guiding me,
as you do.

There were two buses coming:
the first one was crowded, almost to bursting,
"Let's get the next one," I suggested -
as you do.

And so I boarded the second bus,
and went up the stairs,
but you did not follow me through.
I hunted the decks,
passenger-scanning,
interrogating every face:
but I could not see you.

Then I realised that you had gone,
that you had joined the other queue,
and flowed into the spectral horde,
leaving me to ride home alone.
And I fell to the ground, weeping.
As you do.

I thought I was coping so well

I thought I was coping so well.
In the morning, I wake to the daybreaking song:
I re-swallow the knowing
you were gone, and are gone, and will always be gone.
Yet the seas keep on flowing
and the sun will continue to rise
and I'll muddle my way through another today,
unreflected in your eyes.

Returning, I wander through meadows of youth
and stray among tracks of the past;
and out of the shadows, old records replay
in visions and flashbacks,
fast and complete, bone-deep, bittersweet:
as if the truth had been baited, waiting for me
while I was distracted: steadfastly looking
the other way.

An Experience of the Elemental

The sights and sounds of a mid-May morning,
not long after dawn:
every sense stretched out on stalks...
Birdsong bright as the new-painted sky
backlighting the leaves;
Shadows and silhouettes...
The clean air warmed already by
the first kiss of the sun.

Then, looking out to sea,
flickers of light by the shoreline ... diamonds at the horizon ...
Separate islands of shimmer
moving slowly but surely towards each other.

A man in a kayak splits the silky sea between them
and both recede, contract, roll back.
He passes beyond, and when he's gone,
they start to reach out to each other again,
inch by careful inch by inch,
getting faster as they get nearer
as if both are yearning to make this connection.

And then, in a moment, dazzling the eye,
dancing sparks and shining darts suffuse the water -
unable to mark where one begins and the other one ends.

Experiencing the elemental,
the sensual spring and the sea and the sky:
and walking homeward through the churchyard,
the dark smoky odours of the rich, damp earth...

Rhapsody, interrupted

As I walked out one mid-Lockdown morning,
the air was filled with rhapsody.
A miscellany of symphonies
exulted through the canopy.

My ears are in my fingertips –
I stretch out both my arms:
Songs that clean the soul, vein-deep,
vibrating through my palms.

The charm that changes in a heartbeat,
the sound that changes to a wingbeat,
growing louder, thick as thunder,
that propels the deadly hunter.

Relentless, steady, measured,
ever heading for the rise:
before the sweep with blazing lasers,
before the swoop that scoops the prize.

The prey inhale their sorrow,
feathered ruffs a quivered rhythm,
as each anticipates the harrow
come to reap a hapless victim.

And every breath is bating
until death leaves its stain;
And the silent world is waiting
till the band strikes up again.

She was not a statistic

One of 'the vulnerable'- yes,
but not just merely one of anything.
She was only ever herself,
and she sang her own song;
a woman not far from young,
with eyes full of wonder,
and a throaty, flirty giggle
that spread laughter around her.

Her brain carried an impairment
that would never bear repairing,
but more than that, she was
a sister, an aunt, and a daughter,
surrounded by her family,
who fought her corner, ceaselessly,
for her care to be caring,
for her life to be well-lived.

She loved listening to Abba.
Though her limping legs would never dance,
(broken by a life-saving op when she was seventeen) ...
Was she, in her own mind, the Dancing Queen?

So many times,
she defied expectations,
she outfaced calculations
that her body, too weak,
would falter and fail.
She would always prevail.

Her death was not ordained.
She did not die of the afflictions
that had plagued her through life.
She died from a scythe
that razed, panoramic,
that crazed us with panic.

This was the last night.
They called up to say,
'Time to say your goodbyes'.
This time they were right.
We could not hold her hand
as she joined the 'Deaths Listed'.
She was our loved-one, our darling.
She was not a statistic.

The Limitations of Zoom

We are not bone. We are not flesh.
We show an unembodied face,
display a dislocated base;
minds tangle as we breach the miles,
the shy rapport of distant smiles,
to guess what more-than words express
across the bridge of consciousness,
and try to read the signs.

Yes I am here, yet I exist
alone within my separate frame:
and you apart in yours.
Can tendrils reach across this space,
transmit the warmth of fond embrace,
the subtle brush of gentle lips,
linguistic play of fingertips
as your hand touches mine?

Based on only what is seen,
can eyes still speak between the screens?
Can we still reach the tender place
that lies beneath the carapace?
How can we connect without
collisions of the tangible,
the sweet kiss of the visceral,
without corporeality?

Those who crave the mortal spark,
who hunger for the human balm,
the comfort of the calming arm,
stare out with famished hearts.
How can we replace the grace
that feeds between the lines?
Find ways to share our sympathies
in these unfeeling times?

Ode to Autumn Skies

More lustrous than the vernal vault of seamless blue,
The skies of autumn, pied with dreaming hues:
Wings of cloud that stream out fan-wise:
Curds of chalk and woodsmoke plumes.
Wind-blown arms of rolling charcoal,
Haloed by the sun's glow.

Dark-bellied geese from Russia and Siberia
Stretch temperate-seeking skeins
Across the prism's gleaming bow.
Sparkling beads of amber glass
Fall suddenly, like tears, and flow into
Obsidian waves below.

Is beauty's charm diminished by
The thought of passing time?
Is the memory less treasured
When these feathers, at their fringes,
Reflect the dusty tinges
Of frayed summer's sweet decline?

Or is the heart more deeply pierced
When every year embraces, as it must,
The season of descent, and
When the hopes of spring are spent?
When we begin the downward spiral
Into autumn's musty keep?
When the world begins to dwindle
Into winter's looming sleep?

This is how it ends

You tripped just as the world tipped,
in the middle of the season:
before the mothwing dusk of evening,
against the face of time and reason.

How can I fill the space you left me, love?
I feel it still, the warp and weft of love:
we rode the currents and the flows of life,
composed the poetry and prose of life.

At last I find myself believing,
since they told me you were leaving,
that you weren't just going to the shops
or popping out to see your friends,
that summer's loan has overblown:
that this is how it ends.

Why are the birds still singing?

Can anybody tell me
why the birds insist on singing?
Why I hear the songsters calling
through the sad-rose lays of autumn,
the icy blast of winter's horns,
the ancient howling of the storm?

When the nascent spurs of springtime
shone bright as any gleaming gong,
Nature, in anticipation,
set the pulse of summer roaring:
and brood on brood and flock on flock
swarmed skyward with their melodies.

When every tune was soaring,
and every rhythm dance-a-long,
Aurora's blessed light imbued,
from groundlings to the highest rock,
the thrill of syncopation,
the kiss of bliss-filled harmonies.

As short days limp and groan beneath
a brief, crepuscular veneer,
and trees reveal their naked heads -
a shivering, leathered skein of threads -
cold winds still carry trills of cheer,
and hedges bristle shrill with song.

So now, when the earth lies sleeping,
its head folded under its wing,
why do the birds go on cheeping
like they think it's a morning in spring?
In this time of worldwide weeping,
tell me, why do the birds still sing?

An Elegy for Passing Time

I am caught in the unfolding
of twilight's fading dream.
I watch the hues of sunset bruise,
and feel the shadows closing in.

A chattering of scolding song,
of times no longer golden,
and green times that are gone,
breaks out beyond my window.

No promise stakes its case
to fill the vacant space within.
Yet still I sit here waiting
for the next thing to begin.

Mourning Clouds

You felt the warmth of the dawn kiss your wings.
You touched the sky at the moment you fell.
You had more songs that you wanted to sing.
You had more tales that you wanted to tell.

In the skies high above
the railway tracks,
the smoking stacks,
the back-to-backs,
hope never quite dies, love:
the sun will still rise, love.

From dew-sharpened cold,
the darkest night will depart,
the day's clock will re-start.
In the depths of the heart,
mourning clouds will unfold,
and the world will turn gold.

A Small, Brave Flag

Pale prow above the ocean's consternation,
On Christmas Day, one primrose bud unfurled.
A small, brave flag of hope and consolation
To set against the tempests of the world.

PAUL SHAW

These poems follow a general theme of Past, Present and Future. (Though, Eric Morecambe-esque, not necessarily in the right order.)
They tell the tale of life, so far, through the pandemic. The unexpected loss of one of our writing friends; looking back over a kind of year none of us have experienced before; the saviour that is a garden; and what we hope those who come after us will become.
If I have done this well the words will be identifiably personal yet universal.

Afternoon Tea

Beneath the cloudless blue the garden softly busy, hums
Hushed frog, rescued and released, exults amongst the dahlias

Last night's owl sleeps unseen and toads gorge
on unearthed worms
The spade, double-edged, provides and destroys
until muddy boots rest

Tea and old mugs blind the indulgent as drunken bees
blunder unnoticed across the lawn
Quarrelling sparrows dispute a sunflower largesse -
and pay the price

Scything wings whisper the hawk close to snatch life
Pity partners deliverance to dance entwined, and regret accompanies
last sips

The garden's heartbeat steadies
Bloodied. And yet, beautiful

High Summer

Evening sun rides the horizon
Garden colour vivid glows
Begs the sun remain and dance
On delphinium and rose

Night trails his hushing cloak
Bids the flowers sleep
Who sigh and bow their heads
Till a dawn appointment keep

Song Thrush, Robin, Blackbird, Gull
Sound the 'Sunset' call
Tawny Owl stands vigil
Fox begins to call
Dark scents blossom heady soft
Grass awaits the dew
Shrew and Wood mouse eat their fill
Until the day begins anew

The Goldcrest's Nest

The Kinglet's castle, sits insistent as guilt in my palm
A lichen and moss delight prostrated by my incautious hand
Regal yet

The Visitor

Onyx set in green silk, watchful yet haughty
Indifferent to earthlings, tease indigo pearl fruit
Enveloped in magenta in the Glorybower
Settlers from the East alight, cruciform, at twilight
And are gone

Christmas Lights and Roses

The year's candle burns low
Wood cut and fires built
Winter roses cannot be

Yet here they are
Denying the season
Low sun soft in their faces

As day closes her eyes to sleep
Festive lights partner flowers
In a hushed dance into night

2020

From December's peak, chill tears taint the old year
Turn away from what was, or turn towards what will be?
Too stark a choice
Too sharp a cut
A new climb beckons
And we must go; burdened – to greet tomorrow

Resenting Time

I can't be the first to resent time
It gives no hint of what lies in wait
But sprints ahead and drags us in its wake

Indifferent to hopes we hold and plans we make
I can't be the first to resent time
Spectators in events that decide our fate

A chance turn we see too late
Too few clues to the route it will take
I can't be the first to resent time

Wishes

Grandad? What wish shall I make to last forever?
My dear, wish to be bright for it's good to be clever
I could wish to be pretty, if you wouldn't mind?
You already are, but it's better to be kind
Grandad? What wish would you make if it could come true?
That wisdom and caring take root in you

Holding Hands

How far we reach; how much we grow
My grandmother's world was candle lit
I held her hand, as I hold yours

Victoria her Queen and Egypt Britain's war
No telephone nor motor car to speed life on its way
How far we reach; how much we grow

The path ahead is yours to tread
Who you are inside will be your guide
I held her hand, as I hold yours

Make courage your companion
Kindness steer both thought and deed
How far we reach; how much we grow

Your eyes alive, so wide and bright
The past a friend and compass true
I held her hand, as I hold yours

Three centuries we three touch
My grandmother, grandchild and I
How far we reach; how much we grow
I held her hand, as I hold yours

Seed

Growing true and strong
Seeds fed on our tears we trust
Make us immortal

PHIL WELTON

It is said that when we die our whole life flashes across our consciousness. For me, Lockdown has been a kind of suspension of life, with almost nothing to do but reflect.

Like many of us, marooned on our small islands, I have experienced a slow-motion reminder of most of my life – family history, formative experiences, choices made, some regrets, some wonderful memories and intense gratitude for present family, friends and life in general.

And now we have new choices to make.
It is for us to choose who, and how, we want to be while we are here. We've all got to be somebody. We might as well be ourselves.

A Family Visit

Holding her tough skin-and-bone hands,
Cold from long sitting, safe distanced, in our garden,
Now breaking the rules, delinquents both, we grin
And wait as her daughter, my cousin, says goodbye.

I stand beside the car and hold her hands
And watch as tears start in her soft grey eyes.
Who does she weep for, this chilly afternoon?

Her eldest son, in Oz, whose children and
Grandchildren she will likely never hold?
My own late sister of whom she was so fond?
Her sister, my late mother, three years gone?
Or her own life, her childhood, just related?

Little evacuees, trudging up snowbound hills to school.
Her big sister, alive and confident. Herself so shy.
And all those young Welsh boys and girls, forever
Singing to each other across a green, green valley.

Spring Cleaning

I came upon certificates that say I am,
My birth confirmed, recording names and ages,
Mother, Norma (21), father, Tony (23),
Both younger than my own sweet youngest child.
And I, boy, Philip Anthony, June ?? 194?
Norton House, Gloucestershire.
Why on earth Gloucestershire?

I was once shown into the room they rented there,
The garden where I first felt sunshine and fresh air,
The one and only apple of my mother's eye,
The pride of my young father as he made a start.
Nine months within my mother, nine out in the world,
My only private sojourn in their arms and hearts.

Things change. They change remorselessly and in the spring
The idyll ended. Back to crowded in-laws' house.
Victorian childcare rules: "Just let him cry it out,
He's only crying for attention. Leave him, Dear."
Nan picks at Dad, Mum out of sorts with Aunty Grace,
Twin sisters' usurpation of my rightful place
In my own mother's heart and arms, and there I was,
Demoted, not yet two. Mother's little helper.

So house, school, struggle, strife, reunion, then
More children came and life comes round again.
Tony is long gone and Norma late departed.
Life leaves no trace, no memory before
I see my mother, baby at each breast -
A small, grey image, shockingly my first.

Why did I feel so much, my open heart so touched
By my first address, my home from home from birth?
I passed that way just once in 1986.
The lady was so kind. She let me in to look.
I saw the room - a stranger - walked the garden round,
I stared and breathed it in, my origins new-found.

So why so deeply mourn a past long past recall
Save words hand-written on an old official form?
Mind? Body? Spirit? Where might I store traces of
Those nine sweet months of unadulterated love?

FaceTime

At twenty-four and twenty-eight we met.
At twenty-six and thirty we were set.

At twenty-eight you told my Dad "Fuck Off!"
The room went dark
My mother said . . .
"Yes, Tony, please apologise for that remark."

We lived at the frontiers of relationship
And boundaries were there for us to test.
The New Frontier was promising adventure.
New Woman, New Man, our lives would be blessed.

At thirty years and thirty-four we tripped
On kerbstones we could see but not accept.
By thirty-two and thirty-six
Our brave adventure had unravelled into bits.
Pain, bitterness, a wary distance that became
Estrangement and apportioning of blame.

And now, at sixty-seven and seventy-one,
We meet again through screens, and we can trace
The march of time in what we've each become:
Half a lifetime channelled in each face.

Faces changed but voices, really, not,
So many stories each has to convey.
Such friendship still, goodwill and pleasure got
From each success achieved along the way.

So glad we've had occasion to distil
Respect and love from such a bitter cup,
In gratitude for present Pam and Phil,
I thank the Lord Almighty we split up.

Slow Cooking

My turn to cook. Start early. Take it slow.
No hurry. No tight schedule. No demand
Except perhaps some flavour and a change
Of evening meal, the high point of the day.

Our youngest has become the go-to chef,
Instinctively creative, and she loves
The chance to make a difference to our life,
To make a feast from what we have in store.

Of late, the moon has dragged her spirit down.
Our eldest, too, the black dog circles round.
And we must somehow strive to conjure hope
From somewhere near the end of our own rope.

Spaghetti, meat balls and tomato sauce,
A salad on the side, a little wine.
It turned out well - perhaps more salt? Of course
Room for improvement but, that said, divine.

We lift our heads and watch a little news,
How China took two months to open up,
And now one hundred thousand plus lives gone
As Britain took two months before we shut.

Advice from friends, and doctors, is to stop.
Don't watch the news, there's nothing you can do.
Focus on love and friendship, keep the faith,
A thousand plates of love will see us through.

A Shadow Of My Former Self

I'm stood on the deck
While the dog gives the foxes
A wall-bouncing piece of his mind.
Security lights, above and behind me,
Project onto our garden wall
The shadow of my former self.

I've not seen that long-haired shadow
Since 1971 or even '69
On old retaining walls along Perth Road
Where the women lived at number 388.

Or on the staircase wall that took me down
To the Old Student Union where I found
A buzzing Tardis of a basement opening onto
Breughelesque walls, a café, a bar
And tables fit for young men to stomp on.

"We are the fucking Dentals!
Dentals through and through!
We are the fucking Dentals!
Who the fucking hell are you?!!!"
Er…Social Studies actually…Sorry.
Wow. It takes all sorts to fill your teeth.

Or in a quiet carrel or at a library desk,
Once in a while with some work to do,
Fitting it in between the music,
The dramas, the politics, the romance
And did I mention the music?

So why DID we go to the Library?
Why, for years after, was that glossy paper,
Polished wood and cellophane library smell
So very, very aphrodisiac?
I couldn't possibly comment.

Or on the red walls or in the mirrors
Of the Olde Tavern on Hawkhill.
A 'mixed' pub. Uni and Art College.
Why, to this day, has the oil-paint
And canvas smell of an artist's studio
Been so very, very…? I couldn't possibly…

The All-Night Bakery, Greasy Pete's -
Hawkhill had so much to offer
And that shadow on the wall
Will always take me back to
Mock chop suppers, a few pints in The Tav
And a cheese and onion roll at 3.00am.

Alright, Archy. That'll do.
I think the foxes have got the message
At least for an hour or two.
But now I know if I get the yen
To wander down Old Hawkhill again
I can stand on the deck in the dark
With that magic lantern at my back
And follow my shadow through the wall.

The Rose Table

A curious toddler walks under a table
Gracing her grandfather's warm seaside villa.
It stands in the hall, French-polished and smelling
Of old wood and leather, tweed jackets and whisky.

Father, in Florence, finds a round box of leather,
Surprisingly lined with a porcelain so turquoise
Which, one day, will conjure up renaissant memories
Of fragrant tobacco, evoking his presence.

The child gives her elegant mother a gift set
Of round metal coasters, one large and six smaller,
A deep-sea green, splash-streaked with gold, for a message
Expressing so much that the child wants to tell her.

Her sister will give her a box for a keepsake.
Its lid bears an image, a lute-playing cherub,
From a family print first found in the Uffizi,
Now on a forever-house wall rich with colour.

Her daughter's cat drinks from a great vase of flowers,
Upsetting it, spilling large pools of green water
By night to strip layer upon layer of French polish
And lay the wood bare as the old table's birthday.

A close friend will give her an odd metal frog
With an old Chinese coin in its mouth, for abundance.
"I saw this and I thought of you…" says her soul mate.
Such friends will be treasured, their price beyond rubies.

Happy young neighbours will bring, every weekend,
Fresh flowers from their market stall, filling the glass vase
Which stands on the green and gold round metal coaster,
Now safe from that thirsty cat, so long lamented.

Kindly old neighbours will cross the street bearing
A generous glean of large pears from their garden
To ripen around the sweet table's curved edges,
Each fruit with its own petalled bed in the window.

Some day a small child may walk under this table
Beautiful, delicate, freshly French-polished,
Gracing her grandmother's house by the seaside,
Telling of old wood, tobacco and flowers,
Essence of dogs, copper frogs and old boxes,
The fruits of strong friendship, and love in abundance.

Expect The Best But Wear Your Vest

I feel the cold so make damn sure I'm dressed
For all the weather this East Coast can throw
At those who venture out along the Front
And down beyond the pebbles dip their toe.

"I didn't think that there'd be this much wind,"
She shivers, dressed in casual style, quite chic.
"I should have come out walking in the sun.
It was so lovely earlier in the week."

A brisk North-Easter speeds a leaden sky.
The dog trots gamely, sniffing through the flowers.
Wind at our back, we warm up as we try
To manifest the best for us and ours.

These last two years have been a fearful test,
Each of us dragged through fury or despair.
Fault lines we'd known but still left unaddressed
Have ground our dreams almost beyond repair.

Now turning home, we look up and we find
Our brave North wind has chased the clouds away
Revealing what is always there behind
The gifts kind weather brings us every day.

Now facing North, the sun warm on our back,
We take the road home, walking tall, erect,
No longer fixed on what we fear we lack
But crisp and clear on what we can expect.

"Expect The Best," she says and it is true.
So much that's best has come to us of late.
Expect it or we'll blink as it flies through
And miss it, though it's offered on a plate.

There may be times when, sent by ridge or trough,
Onto each life a little rain must fall.
Now, nearing home, we turn to see, far off,
Clouds disappearing, blue sky over all.

To spot it coming on, Expect the Best.
Receive it, net it, share it, let it rest.
Dress warm, in layers easy to divest.
Prepare to greet good fortune aptly dressed!

Resharpening

What makes you happy? Think yourself back there.
Think of your safe space. Put yourself back to where
You were your unedited, unafraid self,
Your razor-sharp edges glinting in the spotlight,
Not yet smoothed or blunted by wear and tear,
Your own self-protective, -effacing, -remoulding,
Your own mind's quasi-parental glare.

So I find myself, as the Talking Heads put it,
Standing atop a mile-high PA speaker,
Rebel yelling, rabble-rousing, my tambourine ringing,
To our cavernous, thunderous opening number.

I find myself on the City Hall stage
Bright, shiny young people all smiling up at me
As I sing to them 'Happy In The Lord', my weird new song
And, by God, I think they've got it!

I find myself at a Canterbury Open Mic
With new uncategorisable songs,
An old man singing a song about youth
And, by God, again, a few young ones have got it!

Give me the Mayfair or Newcastle City Hall
Every day of the week and an Open Mic, Sunday,
Where I was pure me, complete and in tune.
Not an easy-listening cover version of me
But the original, authentic song of myself
Which, with care, social distancing, masks and clean hands,
I fully intend to sing once again.

The Wondrous Fluke

When I look in, there's so much going on.
Too warm, too cold, or happy day, just right.
The air, my clothes, the ground I walk upon,
The quiet dark, the bright, insistent light.

An itch, a tickle or an aching joint,
The cool air in my throat, the warm exhale;
Soft hair against my forehead or the point
Where nerve and tissue find their Holy Grail.

Our journey long, we're looking straight ahead,
Fixed on some future prize, some siren's call
The wondrous fluke, Existence, left unsaid...
The miracle – to simply BE at all.

Time takes its toll. My perfect body fails.
To simply be at all now my delight,
Each new-found flaw bids me unfurl my sails,
Float on Life's breezes and, in time, take flight.

Putting The Bins Out

Rare, now, to be out of doors past nightfall.
Late Sundays the air tells me of old times passing.
Warm scent of trees – a party one young August –
A sweet country cornfield, redolent of harvest,
Two summerhouses, scenes of much sweet music,
And now, tonight, the cool new shirt of school.
Long ago and here and now – September.

JOANNA WEST

During the first lockdown, in March 2020, when leaving our homes was forbidden other than for an hour's exercise or for essential errands, I developed the habit of going on long solitary walks. All of the following poems owe their inception to these walks, when the quiet stillness of this 'new normal' fostered deep reflection, and observation, feelings and memories were heightened.

JOANNA WEST

While the theatres are dark

(Spring 2020)

Where once we trod with commuting feet,
Drumming the street with pounding beat,
Weeds abound in fulsome array.
The dandelion dances centre stage,
Swinging and swaying in a wanton display
Of exuberant, irreverent and bawdy ballet.
She's golden, bold and brash and brazen,
And flaunts her joyous, shameless face
In glorious wild abandon.
While fellow weeds, in less flattering dress,
Scramble to parade in the kerbside line
Or pattern the walls in a slovenly mess
Of riotous slatternly set design.

Confined to our homes, we peep through glass
And eagerly wait for the fun to start
As Nature, the indisputable star,
Readies the set for a comedy sketch.
Gleeful of eye and jaunty of hoof,
The Farmyard Fugitives begin their farce
Tearing off chunks from delectable shrubs
And plundering bulbs blooming in tubs.
They pillage the contents of earthenware pots
And finish their skit in a vegetable plot!
Comic turn done, they flee the scene.
The stage is bare, the curtain falls;
And Nature bows to her last applause.

The Doormat Coup

Mutt is in his usual spot,
Lying on the mat
By the front door -
Which affords him a view
Of the kitchen
And a simmering pot
Of sweet-smelling stew -
When a young tabby cat,
New to the flat
And ignorant yet of its laws,
Comes sashaying up
And nestles in the lap
On his two front paws.
Oh, puzzles Mutt in confused disarray -
And at a loss to know what to do -
Does this little scrap
Have no inkling or clue
That it is I who hold sway
On this special dog's mat?
But young Cat is well versed
In the natural laws
Of the cat versus canine decree
(In matters pertaining to territory)
And, paying no heed to Mutt's dismay,
Embarks instead on a washing spree.

But Mutt, who feels he's quite clean enough,
And this too much of an indignity,
Heaves to his feet with a muttering sigh
And goes to lie
On the floor nearby.
When Mutt's master appears he's surprised to see
His dog not on guard in front of the door
But looking downhearted, slumped on the floor.
'Cat got the better of you, did she?'
Mutt, much affronted, is quick to respond:
'Just a chit of a cat
Get the better of me?
Tomorrow you'll see
What changes there'll be
Once I've taught her the laws of the mat.'

The Peregrine

The peregrine falcon comes swooping down,
Deadly eye hooded in a hangman's crown,
Wings dark as a widow's gown -
Daylight shadow of menacing night.
His stoop as fast as a missile flight,
He scores the bird-busy sky below,
Scattering pigeons, gulls and a carrion crow;
He soars over tops of distant trees,
Silencing the song of a mistle thrush.
Then, flying low near a meadow stream,
He slows his speed, and comes to rest
Between some black-topped rushes
And a fledglings' nest.

The horse chestnut tree is dead

This magnificent beast will no more
Shake its lush green mane in rage, and roar
At our Kentish fierce north-easterly.
Quite when it was that it ceased to be
Nobody knows - which is sad but true -
Though general opinion is of the view
That it was in high summer - or during the snow -
When it would last have felt the east wind blow.
While we debate, contest and argue the toss,
And weep for wildlife's habitat loss,
We try and recall if there were conkers or not,
Or if there'd been on the bark bleeding canker or rot.
Yet it's only now, when we're well into spring
(Hindsight would be such a wonderful thing!)
And we notice there's been no rebirth,
That we bother to stop and examine its girth.
And so, too late, we shed our tears
For this tree that lived one hundred years,
Giving creatures sanctuary and children fun,
Sheltering us all from the wind, rain and sun.
And we grieve for the leaves of its lush green shade
Where, deep in their midst, its end song played.

Don't bother me now

Across the sweep of the marshland flats
Rolling sea mist blots my path
In clouds of drifting monochrome.
Wrapped in folds of damp and murk,
Silence my only company,
My thoughts and I freely roam,
Shrouded in ghostly secrecy.
While, under her veil of fallen sky,
Nature slumbers, spent and still,
And troubles not my pensive eye.
So, thus, I wander in deep reverie,
Allowing my thoughts to lead the way -
Past leafless trees and unsown fields,
Along an ancient byway -
Until I reach and crest a hill
Where, taking now the downward trail,
The sea-fog thins, and thins some more,
And I find myself in a little while
Bathed in the sun's embrace.

Half-closing my eyes to its glinting rays,
I dream ahead to summer days -
To travelling fairs and garden fetes,
And skies of blistering-blue -
When all the world comes down to stay
And all the town comes out to play...

And I just want to say:
Go, go! Don't bother me now
With your warm caress and seductive ways,
Let me linger yet awhile
In peaceful winter solitude.
For when I step up to that summer stage
(Oh, but how should I prepare?)
And, lost for words, I stand and stare
In the glare of your burning gaze -
With people watching here and there -
How will I know what part to play?
Will someone prompt me from the wings?
Will someone tell me what to say?
How will I know to act as I ought
After being so long in solitary thought?

The Ravages of Time

Her skin is parchment thin.
Flesh falls away from bone.
Yet time's cruellest ravages are wrought unseen,
Where age, conniving, unpicks her story's seams
And memories unravel, thread by thread,
Leaving a jumble strewn with nothingness.

But deep in the ruins of these reels undone,
An echo begins to stir,
A hint of a woman from eons ago.
Though do not blink,
Or she'll go.

Shadow Thought

Away from me
My shadow is malevolent,
Running out at me unexpectedly
When I'm deep in abstract thought;
So that my heart, in outrage, leaps at the bars
Of its bony enclosure
And knocks my breath from its leisurely path,
Which then feels the need to right itself
With a frenzied burst of speed.
And, when the beam of the culprit lamp
Has fallen far behind,
And my heart has quietened down again
And my breath has ceased to rush,
I try, in vain,
To grasp the tail
Of the serpent thread
Attached to my previous thought,
Before it slithers away
Through the blown-in rubbish
And into the shadowlands.

Lockdown Blues

Under the weary February dusk
The deserted streets lie eerie.
No feral cat, nor barking dog,
Nor yet another soul,
Accompanies me on my solitary stroll.
I wander through the darkening gloom,
Along the ancient contraband trail,
To the clustered cottages and narrow streets
Where smugglers used to dwell.
The quarter is quiet with a ghostly aura
Without its meandering tourists,
And doors and shutters in greys and blues
Loom before me in bodeful hues.

I turn away from these brooding lanes
And wend my way to the esplanade
Where, alone on its patch hugging the shore,
The Grand Hotel stands sombre and grave.
No longer do lovers in sea-view rooms
Hold hands and romance on a balcony;
No laughter spills out from the bar below,
Nor glasses clink under night-starred glow.
The bar and the rooms now lie lonely as tombs,
Shrouded in silence, blind to the sea.

How still our town is, its lifeblood drawn;
Bled of all colour, inert, forlorn.
I sit on the seawall in downcast mood
And the bitter raw chill sits down with me.
But the rhythms, unchanged, of the wind and the sea,
The crash on the shingle, the spray in my hair,
The tang on my lips from the salt-torn air,
Dispel those thoughts that weigh and intrude;
My spirits are lightened, my soul is soothed.

Memory Train

On platform one, at your beginning,
An empty carriage awaits
The slapping of your infant rear
And your first indignant shout.
Alone you board the stopping train,
The vacant seats reserved
For memories now bestirring
Along the virgin track.

The train, impatient, departs at last,
The whistle is blown; the adventure starts.
Here comes a station and memories young
Stumble and trip in their rush to get on.
In a scrum they race to the seat at the front
To leave an imprint where yet there's none,
And not be forsaken nor ever forgot
On the journey unfurling before them.

The train makes haste and hurtles on
Through raging storms, and brooding woods
Steeped in the shadows of youth.
Then slows its speed on a serpentine climb
To find a valley bejewelled
With silvered pools, where memories lie
Shimmering beneath a sparkling sky
Of deep azure, and frosted peaks.

But, inside, the mountain's tunnel is thick with black,
The glow of light too far ahead
To thin the cloying dark.
You hold your cherished memories close.
And when, in time, the train emerges,
Though the landscape's not the same,
The charcoal clouds are fading
And a shy sun feels softly warm
Against the sooted glass.

Ocean going

O, to be an ocean-going ship,
Free to sail the seas,
And leave in your wake the little craft
That gnaw at your side like fleas.

O, to be in the ocean air,
Away from the cares and pain
That bind you to this cloying land
With a soft-wrapped ball and chain.